RYKER
BLUEPRINT
PRESS

Dedication

To my two boys, Ramzes Garza and Easton Gomez,
You were the spark that lit this series.

This was written with the faith and love I've carried since the day each of you were born.

Everything good I create carries both your names.

One story, one promise, and one book of the Bible at a time.

With all my faith and love,
Mom

God wants us to shine bright just like little lights in the world!

But in order to shine, we need His words tucked into our hearts.

We learn His words by reading the Bible and its many stories.

Each book helps us grow strong, brave, and kind, just like God wants to be!

Here are four of His stories...

Table of Contents:

Job's Big Test
A Story from the Book of Job

Once upon a time, in a faraway land, there lived a kind and faithful man named Job. Job loved God with all his heart. Every day, he gave thanks for his family, his animals, and the wonderful life he had.

Job had seven sons and three daughters. He owned thousands of sheep, camels, and other animals. Everyone in the town knew Job was the richest man around, but he was also the kindest. He shared his blessings and helped those in need.

One day, something very mysterious happened. High up in heaven, God was talking to the angels. But someone else was there too – it was Satan. Satan did not believe Job loved God for the right reasons. He said, "Job only loves You because his life is easy. Take everything away, and he will stop praising You!"

God knew Job's heart and said, "Job is faithful. You may test him, but you cannot hurt him."

Suddenly, Job's happy life changed. One day, his servants came running with sad news.

"Job, your animals are gone! Your fields are empty!" Then, even sadder news came – a great storm had knocked down the house where his children were, and they were gone too.

Job felt his heartbreak. He cried many tears, but he did not stop loving God. He said, "The Lord gave me everything, and now He has taken it away. Blessed be the name of the Lord."

Satan was surprised. He thought for sure Job would give up, but Job did not. So, Satan asked God again, "If Job loses his health, he will turn away from You."
God said, "You may test him, but you must not take his life."

Poor Job became very sick. His skin hurt, and he felt weak. Even his friends did not understand. They told Job he must have done something wrong. But Job knew he had always tried to do good. He did not understand why these bad things were happening, but he still trusted God.

Day after day, Job prayed to God. He asked questions, but he never stopped believing that God was good. One day, God answered Job from a mighty whirlwind. God reminded Job that He had made the whole world – the stars, the sea, and every living thing. God knew all things, even when Job did not understand.

Job realized that God was in control, and that was enough for him. He said, "I know that You can do all things. My heart trusts in You."

Because Job stayed faithful, God blessed him again. He gave Job even more than he had before – more animals, more fields, and even a new family. Job lived a long, happy life, always trusting in God's goodness.

Remember, even when life is hard, God is always with us. Like Job, we can trust God, knowing He loves us and has a good plan for our lives. When we hold on to faith, blessings can follow in ways we never expect!

Songs From The Heart
A Story from the Book of Psalms

Long ago, there was a young shepherd boy named David. David loved to sing and play his harp while watching over his sheep. As he looked at the bright stars, the rolling hills, and the gentle streams, his heart filled with joy. Whenever David felt happy or sad, he would talk to God through songs and prayers.

David knew that God was always with him. Whether the sun was shining or storms were coming, David would sing, "The Lord is my shepherd; I have everything I need."

As David grew up, life became harder. He faced many troubles, but he never stopped singing to God. When he felt scared, he prayed, "When I am afraid, I will trust in You." When he was thankful, he sang, "Give thanks to the Lord, for He is good. His love lasts forever."

One day, David had to face a giant named Goliath. Everyone else was too afraid, but David trusted God to protect him. With a small stone and a big faith, David defeated the giant! After that day, David praised God even more, singing, "With God, all things are possible!"

Years later, David became a king. Even with all his power, he still knew that God was the true King over everything. He wrote songs to remind people to praise God. "Let everything that has breath praise the Lord!" he declared

Sometimes, David made mistakes. When he did, he prayed to God for forgiveness. "Create in me a clean heart, O God," he asked. And because God is loving and kind, He forgave David and helped him follow the right path again.

David's songs became part of a special book called the Psalms. These songs help us remember that God listens when we pray. Whether we are happy, sad, scared, or thankful, we can always talk to Him.

When you feel joyful, you can sing like David, "This is the day the Lord has made; let us rejoice and be glad in it!" When you feel worried, you can remember, "The Lord is my light and my salvation; whom shall I fear?"

PSALMS

David's songs are still with us today. They remind us that God loves us, cares for us, and is always near. No matter what happens, we can lift our hearts to Him in prayer and praise.

Remember, just like David, you can talk to God anytime. Whether you are happy, sad, or afraid, God is always ready to listen. Your prayers are like songs that bring joy to His heart!

God's Love Never Ends

A Story from the Book of Lamentations

A long time ago, there was a city called Jerusalem. It was a beautiful city where people worshipped God. But one day, the city was filled with sadness. The people had forgotten to follow God's ways, and their city was broken and quiet.

A man named Jeremiah walked through the empty streets. His heart felt heavy because he loved the people and the city. Tears fell from his eyes as he whispered, "How lonely the city is now." He felt sad but knew he could talk to God about his feelings.

Even when everything seemed dark, Jeremiah remembered something very important—God's love never ends! He said, "The Lord's love never stops. His kindness never comes to an end. Every morning, He shows us new mercy."

When Jeremiah was scared, he prayed to God. When he was sad, he told God how he felt. And when he needed hope, he remembered that God is always good. He said, "The Lord is good to those who trust in Him."

The people of Jerusalem had made mistakes, but Jeremiah knew that God still loved them. He trusted that one day, God would bring joy back to the city. Even when we make mistakes, God is always ready to forgive us and help us start again.

Sometimes, we all feel sad or worried. But like Jeremiah, we can remember that God's love is bigger than our troubles. His kindness is new every day, and He is always with us. Whenever you feel down, you can say like Jeremiah, "The Lord is my hope, so I will trust in Him."

And just like God brought hope back to Jerusalem, He can bring hope to our hearts, too.

When you feel sad, remember that God loves you. His kindness never ends, and He is always there to listen. No matter what happens, you can trust in His love and find hope again!

God's Wonderful Promise
A Story from the Book of Revelation

A long time ago, God gave a special message to a man named John. John loved Jesus and wanted everyone to know about His love. One day, while John was on an island, God showed him amazing things about the future.

John saw a beautiful vision of heaven! There were streets of gold, sparkling like glass, and 12 shining gates made of pearl. The base of the city walls was decorated with every kind of precious stone. It was the most wonderful place, filled with joy and light.

In heaven, John saw Jesus, the King of Kings and the Lord of Lords. And Jesus said, "Do not be afraid. I am the First and the Last. I was dead, but now I am alive forever!" John knew that Jesus had won over all darkness and that His love never ends.

KING OF KINGS
LORD OF LORDS

John also saw angels singing praises to God. They said, "Holy, holy, holy is the Lord God Almighty!" Everyone in heaven was happy because God's goodness was everywhere.

But John also saw that life on earth would not always be easy. Sometimes there would be hard days, but Jesus promised to always be with those who love Him. Jesus said, "I am coming soon. Hold on to what is good."

John saw a new heaven and a new earth, where there would be no more sadness, tears, pain, or even death. God said, "I will make everything new!" In this wonderful place, God would live with His people forever, and nothing terrible would ever happen again.

HOLY, HOLY HOLY IS THE LORD GOD ALMIGHTY!
HOLY, HOLY HOLY IS THE LORD GOD ALMIGHTY!

Jesus' promise is for everyone who believes in Him. He invites us to be part of His forever home, where there is joy, peace, and love that never ends.

Whenever you feel worried, remember Jesus' words: "I am with you always." And one day, He will make everything perfect and new. God and Jesus have a wonderful promise for you! They are always with you, and one day, they will make everything new and perfect. You can trust their love forever!

Thinking about homeschooling?

Get support, resources, and connection in our private homeschool community.

Scan the code to join our community and let's figure it out together.

Smart money habits start young.

The Easton Learns series teaches kids the money lessons schools forgot through fun, easy-to-understand stories.

📚 Scan the QR code to explore more books in the series.

Follow Heaven's Amen On Facebook!